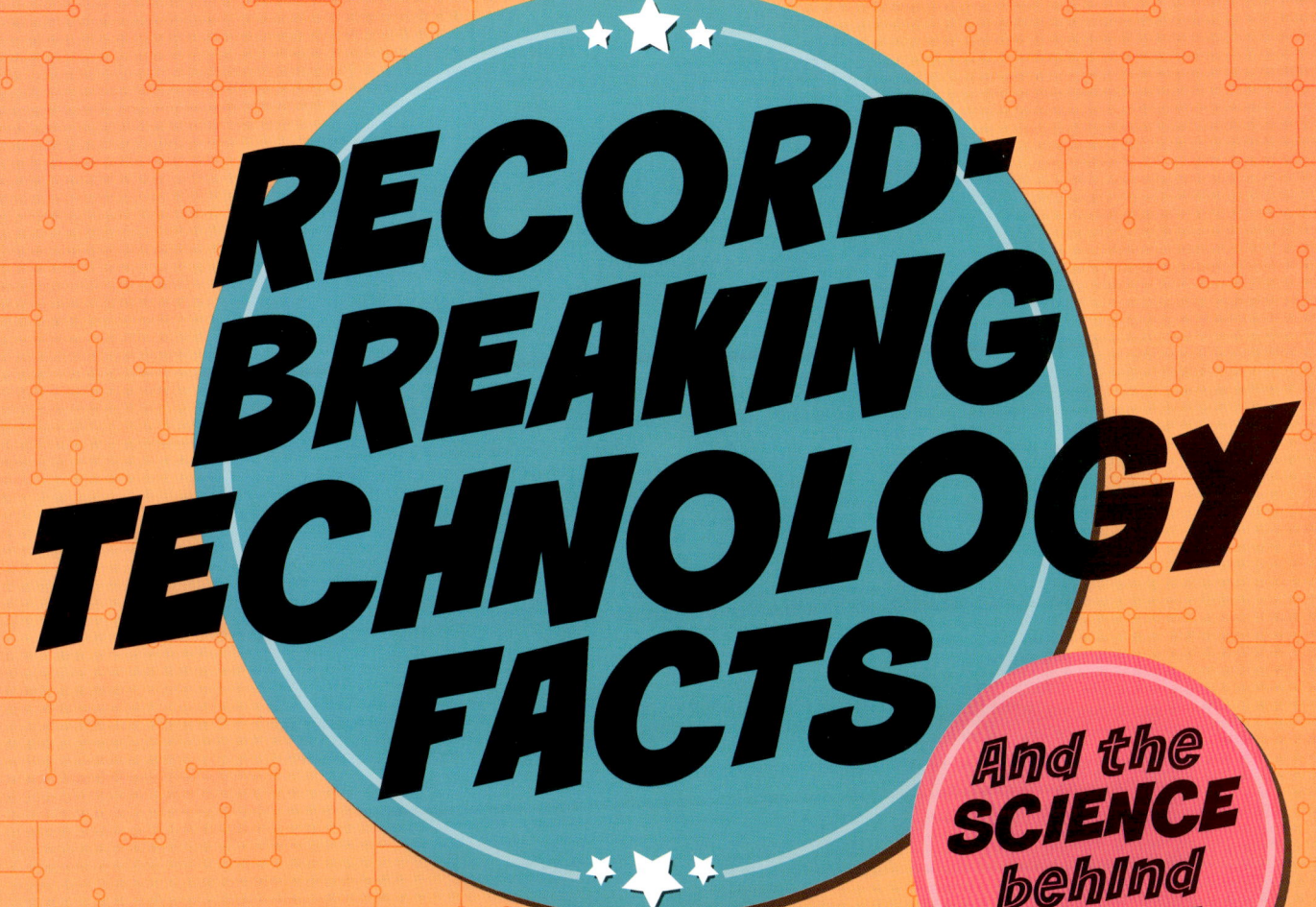

Record-Breaking Technology Facts

And the SCIENCE behind them!

Izzi Howell

WAYLAND

First published in Great Britain in 2026
by Hodder & Stoughton
Copyright © Hodder & Stoughton, 2026
Produced for Wayland by

All rights reserved.

Editor: Izzi Howell
Designer: Clare Nicholas

HB ISBN: 978 1 5263 2971 4
PB ISBN: 978 1 5263 2972 1

Wayland
An imprint of
Hachette Children's Group
Part of Hodder & Stoughton
Carmelite House
50 Victoria Embankment
London EC4Y 0DZ

An Hachette UK Company
www.hachette.co.uk
www.hachettechildrens.co.uk

The authorised representative in the EEA is Hachette Ireland, 8 Castlecourt Centre, Dublin 15, D15 XTP3, Ireland (email: info@hbgi.ie)

MIX
Paper | Supporting responsible forestry
FSC® C104740

Printed in Dubai

Picture acknowledgements:
IBM: Reprint Courtesy of IBM Corporation © 2024 28b; NASA: NASA Johnson cover; Lauren Dauphin, NASA Earth Observatory 15t, NASA/Johns Hopkins APL/Steve Gribben 17t, NASA, ESA, CSA, and STScI 18, 19l, NASA GSFC/CIL/Adriana Manrique Gutierrez 19r, 23b, NASA Johnson 26, 27t, 30b; Shuttestock: Peteri, Crevis, Jose Luis Stephens, CobraCZ, The Yudel Media, patruflo, Legran48D cover, Anusorn Nakdee 3t and 24-25, Arsgera 4-5 and 30t, OPIS Zagreb 5t, scworkspace vector art 5b, PeopleImages.com - Yuri A 6, Svetlana Rey 7l, Kitichan 7r, Vlad Klok 8, Solodov Aleksei 9r, Bradipoo 10l, Forance 10r-11 and 31, karanik yimpat 11b, 12, Cali6ro 13b, Henryk Sadura 14, Shmakova_creative 15b, Bobb Klissourski 17b, Poltavska Yuliia 19t, 13FTStudio 21, HeyClipart 23t, Prostock-studio 24l, ghrzuzudu 24b, Gorodenkoff 25r, Oxsana Chumakova 27b, gd_project 28c, Dilok Klaisataporn 29t, Ique Perez 29c, Shutterstock-Pixelsquid 29b; University of Maine 22; Wikimedia: Freggs 3b and 16-17, Raimond Spekking / CC BY-SA 4.0 9l, OLCF at ORNL 13t, Saruno Hirobano 28t; Wyss Institute at Harvard University cover and 20.

All design elements from Shutterstock.

The website addresses (URLs) included in this book were valid at the time of going to press. However, it is possible that contents or addresses may have changed since the publication of this book. No responsibility for any such changes can be accepted by either the author or the publisher.

All facts and statistics were correct at the time of press.

MEASUREMENTS

Keep track of all the measurements in the book with this handy guide!

cm = centimetre
m = metre
km = kilometre
g = gram
kg = kilogram

Contents

Too big to fly? 4
Champion clicks 6
Deep, deep down 8
Solid and sturdy 10
Prize processors 12
Let it shine 14
(Nearly!) supersonic speed 16
Seeing in space 18
Fabulous fliers 20
King of the printers 22
Whizzy WiFi 24
Super satellite 26
More incredible technology records 28
Glossary 30
Further information 31
Index 32

TOO BIG TO FLY?

LARGEST AIRCRAFT

Can you imagine a plane big enough to carry a wind turbine blade?! At 84 m long and 88 m wide across its wings, the **ANTONOV AN-225 MRIYA** is the largest aircraft ever built. It's also the only aircraft of its size in the world, making it extra special.

Antonov An-225

Standard plane

BIG PLANE, BIG CARGO

The Antonov An-225 was originally designed and built to carry spacecraft in the 1980s, but is now used to transport objects that are too large to fit in standard planes. It's even strong enough and big enough to carry heavy military tanks and diesel locomotives!

The Antonov An-225 has six engines to produce enough power to propel the plus-sized plane *and* its heavy cargo through the air. Most regular planes only have two to four engines.

Certain features such as a back door and an extendable ramp have been removed from the plane to reduce its overall weight so that it can carry its heavy loads.

🌬 NICE AND SMOOTH

The Antonov An-225's twin tail helps to stabilise the plane during flight. Without the twin tail, the heavy weight of the plane and its load would have majorly disturbed the air around the plane. This could have created serious turbulence for other aircraft flying through the same area.

The floor of the plane is reinforced to support the extra weight of the plane's cargo.

The cargo hold of the Antonov An-225 is large enough to carry 80 cars!

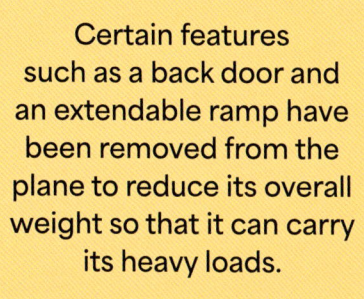

🏆 DID YOU KNOW?

The Antonov An-225 holds an incredible 240 aviation records, including heaviest aircraft and largest wingspan. It also carried the heaviest single piece of air cargo – a generator for a power plant that weighed nearly 190,000 kg (that's as much as around 30 *Tyrannosaurus rex*!)

No way!

CHAMPION CLICKS

MOST VISITED WEBSITE TYPE

With millions of visits every minute, **SEARCH ENGINES** such as Google and Baidu are the most visited type of website. As a key tool in finding information online, it's no surprise that search engines are so popular. Let's take a peek at the programming that allows them to come up with helpful results so quickly.

Search engines use web crawler software to constantly browse the Internet, creating a searchable index of the information on each website.

When you search for something using a search engine, a sophisticated algorithm matches your search terms to the content in its index and creates a list of websites for you to visit. The algorithm also considers your search history, location and other details.

SEARCH SECRETS

Did you know that there are hacks to make your search engine results even more accurate? To remove a word from your search, simply add the minus sign before it. So, if you're looking for an eggless cake recipe, simply search for cake recipe -eggs.

To search for a whole phrase rather than individual words, place speech marks around the phrase. For example, if you type in **oldest cat**, you might get results for cats in general, but if you search for **"oldest cat"**, you'll only get results showing the most ancient moggies around!

DID YOU KNOW?

Some search engines allow users to:
★ roll a die (search roll a die)
★ flip a coin (search flip a coin)
★ and even play a game of solitaire (search solitaire)!

Major search engines, such as Google, have huge numbers of algorithms working on searches all the time, so people's results are usually available within less than a second!

USEFUL DATA

Search engine data can be analysed to get more information about global trends and events. During the COVID-19 pandemic, scientists used data from people's searches for symptoms to help understand how variants of the virus with different symptoms were spreading and replacing each other.

DEEP, DEEP DOWN

DEEPEST SUBMERSIBLE

The *DEEPSEA CHALLENGER* can explore the mysterious depths of Challenger Deep in the Pacific Ocean, the deepest known point of the seabed. The submersible was carefully designed to withstand the extreme conditions deep underwater.

DID YOU KNOW?

Challenger Deep is estimated to be about 10,935 m deep, which is more than the height of Mount Everest!

More than me? How rude!

Deepsea Challenger is totally reliant on battery power during a dive. It holds 70 battery packs that power the submersible's life support system, lights, cameras and thrusters to help the submersible move around at the bottom of the seabed.

A 500 kg weight helps *Deepsea Challenger* sink to the bottom of Challenger Deep. This weight can then be released to allow the submersible to rise back up to the surface.

The pilot (and only crew member!) of *Deepsea Challenger* is protected in a steel-walled sphere. Inside the sphere are controls to move the submersible around the seabed.

⬆⬇ MAKING MATERIALS

About 70 per cent of *Deepsea Challenger* is made out of a type of foam that was created specifically for this project. Its composition allows the submersible to float as it rises back up to the surface but also withstand the pressure deep underwater.

📞 SAFETY AT SEA

For safety, the *Deepsea Challenger* is in constant contact with a support ship up on the surface. The submersible sends out sound signals which the support ship picks up with a hydrophone (an underwater microphone).

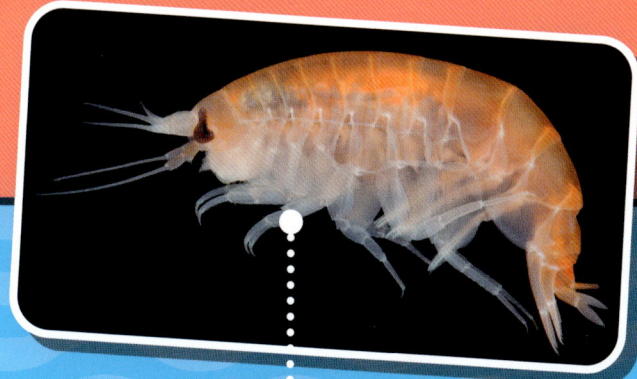

Deepsea Challenger contained cameras and equipment to take images and samples from the bottom of Challenger Deep. The pilot observed small shrimp-like animals on the seabed, but not much else!

SOLID AND STURDY

STRONGEST SUBSTANCE

Forget diamonds - **GRAPHENE** is stronger than any other material, either naturally occurring or made by humans! This strange but incredible substance developed by scientists is 200 times stronger than steel but thinner and lighter than a sheet of paper.

DID YOU KNOW?

The first scientists to discover graphene extracted it from graphite by sticking tape on graphite and peeling it off to remove tiny flakes. They repeated this process on the flakes until they were left with a single layer of graphene!

The secret to graphene's strength is its regular, repeated structure with strong bonds between its atoms.

It's hard to imagine, but graphene is made up of just one single layer of carbon atoms. These atoms are arranged in a hexagonal structure.

SUPERSTAR SUBSTANCE

Graphene also has many other prize-winning properties. It's the thinnest 3D (three-dimensional) material (although it can still be seen with the naked eye!) and conducts electricity better than any other material at room temperature.

According to scientists, a hammock made up of one square metre of graphene would be strong enough to support one average cat weighing about 4 kg. The hammock itself would only weigh as much as one of the cat's whiskers!

GRAPHENE GOALS

Scientists are experimenting with using graphene in many different types of technology. They believe it could help improve battery duration, purify and remove pollution from water and even be used on tiny sensors that travel through your bloodstream to monitor your health.

Tennis rackets made with graphene are already on the market! The company that makes the rackets claims that they are stronger and lighter than standard rackets.

PRIZE PROCESSORS

MOST POWERFUL SUPERCOMPUTER

It may not look much like the computers we use every day but the bundles of cables shown opposite (officially known as the **FRONTIER SUPERCOMPUTER**) actually make up the world's fastest and most powerful supercomputer!

The Frontier supercomputer contains nearly 9,500 CPUs (central processing units) and nearly 38,000 GPUs (graphics processing units) - your computer at home probably has just one of each.

🧪 POWER WITH A PURPOSE

The Frontier supercomputer is mostly used by scientists to analyse and compare data. The supercomputer can predict results far faster than scientists can carry out experiments, which saves them time and resources.

Frontier is about one million times more powerful than a home computer. It's capable of carrying out a staggering 1.1 billion billion operations *per second*.

Scientists have used the Frontier supercomputer to run complex computer programs that simulate how clouds form and study how they may be affected by climate change.

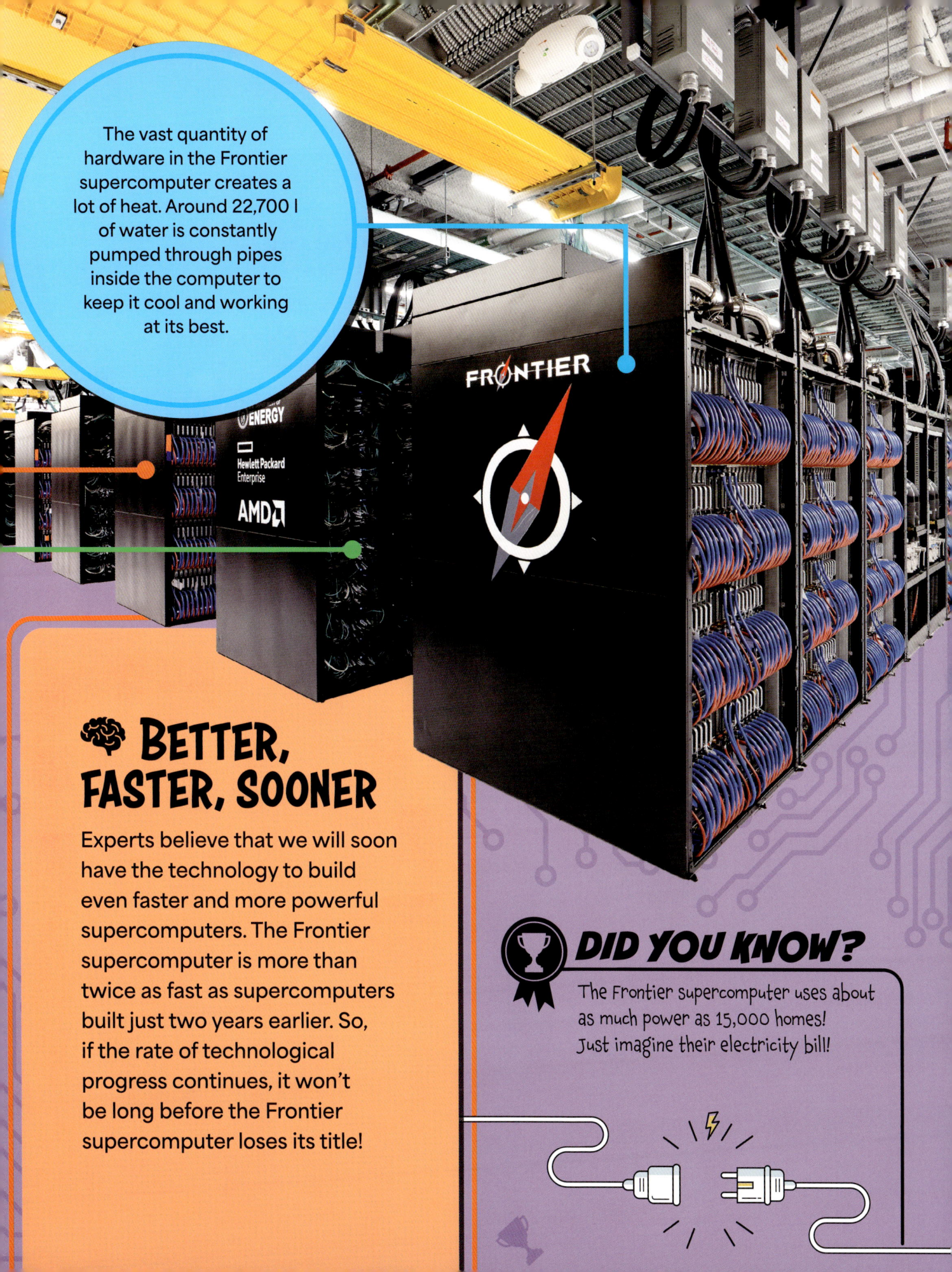

The vast quantity of hardware in the Frontier supercomputer creates a lot of heat. Around 22,700 l of water is constantly pumped through pipes inside the computer to keep it cool and working at its best.

🧠 BETTER, FASTER, SOONER

Experts believe that we will soon have the technology to build even faster and more powerful supercomputers. The Frontier supercomputer is more than twice as fast as supercomputers built just two years earlier. So, if the rate of technological progress continues, it won't be long before the Frontier supercomputer loses its title!

🏆 DID YOU KNOW?

The Frontier supercomputer uses about as much power as 15,000 homes! Just imagine their electricity bill!

LET IT SHINE

BIGGEST SOLAR PARK

The massive, metallic mass of **BHADLA SOLAR PARK** in India could easily be mistaken for a giant lake, but it's actually 10 million solar panels! At 56 square km (one fifth of the size of Edinburgh, Scotland!), it's the world's largest solar park.

☀ ELECTRIC CHARGE

Solar panels are made up of photovoltaic cells, which are made of materials that produce an electric charge when exposed to sunlight. This electricity then travels along wires to the electric grid, which supplies energy to homes and businesses.

⚡ PANEL POWER

One photovoltaic cell only produces a small amount of electricity, but lots of cells in lots of panels can make a lot of power! Several solar panels can produce enough electricity to power a house, while a solar park the size of Bhadla generates enough electricity to power 4.5 million homes.

Mini solar panels can be used to power small machines in the street, such as this parking meter.

In order to produce solar energy, you need sunshine ... and lots of it! The Bhadla Solar Park was built in a desert where the skies are clear and sunny every day.

However, dust from the sandy desert can collect on the panels, making them less efficient. As there is so little water in the desert, engineers found a water-free solution - tiny robots that clean the panels!

Scientists are planning to use satellite imaging to identify which solar panels need to be cleaned, so that they can save time and resources by only sending robots to dirty panels.

DID YOU KNOW?

If we covered 50 per cent of the world's rooftops in solar panels, we'd generate enough electricity to power the whole world!

(NEARLY!) SUPERSONIC SPEED

FASTEST LAND VEHICLE

If you're running late for school, you might want to catch a lift in the **THRUSTSSC**! This vehicle holds the land speed record and can reach speeds of 1,228 km per hour. At that speed, you might even beat your teachers to class!

The ThrustSSC is the only land vehicle ever to break the sound barrier. This is a massive increase in air resistance that objects experience as they get close to moving at the speed of sound.

Reaching super speed *and* overcoming the force of the sound barrier requires some serious engine power. The ThrustSSC uses two jet engines designed for a jet fighter aircraft.

The curved shape of the ThrustSSC made it streamlined so that it could move through the air without any additional air resistance, as this would have slowed the vehicle down.

⏱️ SUPERSONIC SPEED

The ThrustSSC came very close to moving at the speed of sound (1,236 km per hour). Objects that can travel faster than the speed of sound (such as certain aircraft and spacecraft) are known as supersonic. So, despite the SSC in its name, which stands for 'Super Sonic Car', the ThrustSSC is actually an *almost*-supersonic vehicle!

🚀 ZOOMING THROUGH SPACE

The ThrustSSC may be the fastest land vehicle, but it's nowhere near the fastest object ever built! That record is held by the Parker Solar Probe, which was created by NASA to observe the Sun's atmosphere. It's capable of a top speed of 690,000 km per hour, which allows it to quickly get close enough to take measurements and then zoom off before it's damaged by the Sun's radiation.

The Parker Solar Probe's sun shield will protect it from some of the Sun's radiation, but not all of it, so it needs to get in and out very quickly!

🏆 DID YOU KNOW?

The ThrustSSC's engines consume about 18 l of fuel per second when the vehicle is at top speed!

That's it! I'm not giving you any more!

Seeing in Space

Most Powerful Space Telescope

Space telescopes have always provided us with a superior view of our universe than telescopes on Earth, as there's no pesky atmosphere out there to get in the way! However, with the launch of the super-powerful JAMES WEBB SPACE TELESCOPE, we can now see space better than ever before.

Invisible Light

Unlike the telescopes we typically use on Earth, which observe visible light, the James Webb Space Telescope captures infrared light, which is invisible to the human eye. This makes it easier for it to pick up light from early galaxies and stars.

Back in Time

Scientists are particularly interested in using the James Webb Space Telescope to observe light released by some of the first stars and galaxies. This light has been travelling for billions of years to reach our little corner of our solar system. When it is picked up by a telescope, it will give us a glimpse into the history of the universe.

The James Webb Space Telescope captured this image of thousands of galaxies deep in space, as they were 4.6 billion years ago.

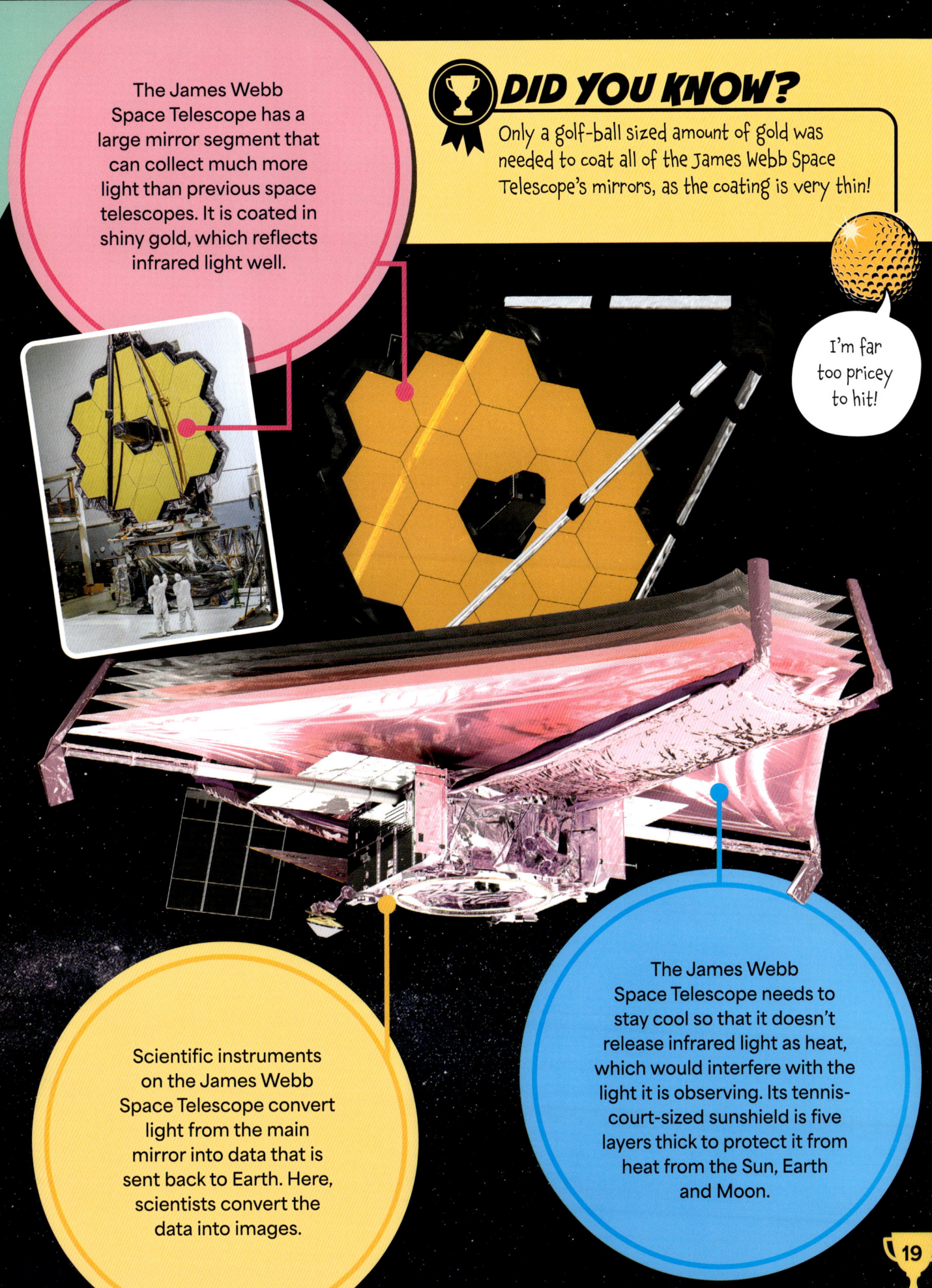

The James Webb Space Telescope has a large mirror segment that can collect much more light than previous space telescopes. It is coated in shiny gold, which reflects infrared light well.

DID YOU KNOW?

Only a golf-ball sized amount of gold was needed to coat all of the James Webb Space Telescope's mirrors, as the coating is very thin!

I'm far too pricey to hit!

Scientific instruments on the James Webb Space Telescope convert light from the main mirror into data that is sent back to Earth. Here, scientists convert the data into images.

The James Webb Space Telescope needs to stay cool so that it doesn't release infrared light as heat, which would interfere with the light it is observing. Its tennis-court-sized sunshield is five layers thick to protect it from heat from the Sun, Earth and Moon.

FABULOUS FLIERS

SMALLEST HUMAN-MADE WINGSPAN

Tiny wings are everywhere in nature, but much harder for humans to recreate! However, skilled engineers have developed the **ROBOBEE** — a miniature robot with a wingspan of just 3 cm!

3 cm
the wingspan of the Robobee

A tiny control system instructs each wing independently so that the Robobee can steer and change direction as it flies.

The Robobee weighs less than one-tenth of gram thanks to its wafer-thin wings and lightweight body made of plastic and carbon fibre.

The Robobee flies by using artificial muscles to flap its wings around 120 times per second. Electricity is used to make the 'muscles' contract and relax.

🐝 ROBOT SWARM

Eventually, the creators of the Robobee hope that they will be able to program the robots to behave like real bees and work together as a group. They could be used in search and rescue operations to explore areas in an organised way or even to artificially pollinate crops.

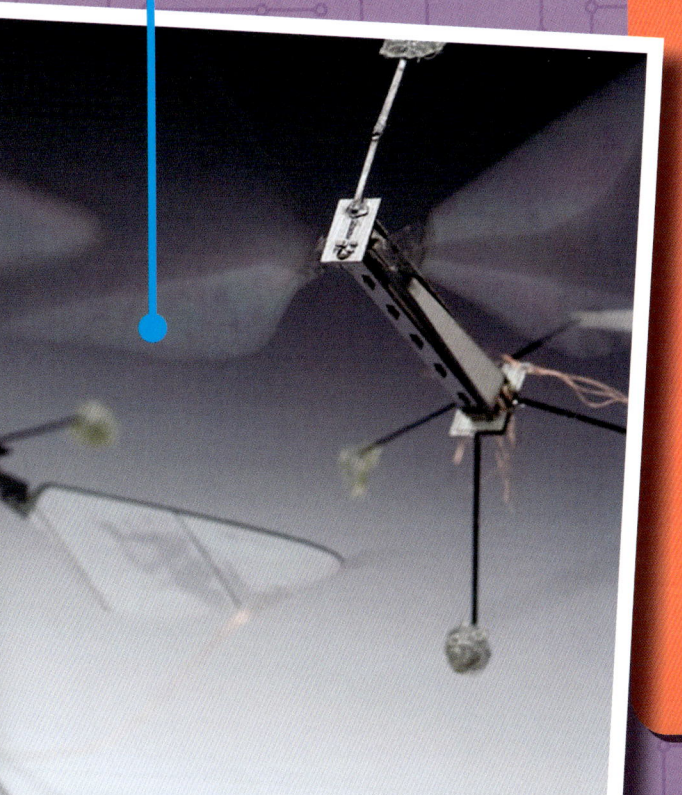

UNLIKELY INSPIRATION

It's very hard to build robots at such a small scale as standard parts, such as screws and gears, aren't made in such tiny sizes! Instead of using these parts, the designers of the Robobee created a new method of construction inspired by children's pop-up books. They cut out the pieces from flat sheets and then folded and glued them together.

DID YOU KNOW?

Some Robobees have been adapted so that they can swim underwater!

King of the Printers

LARGEST 3D PRINTER

If you could 3D print anything, what would it be? A toy? A figurine? How about a boat or a house?! The **FoF 1.0 3D PRINTER**, designed by and located at the University of Maine, USA, can do just that, printing massive objects up to 29 m long. That's as long as a blue whale!

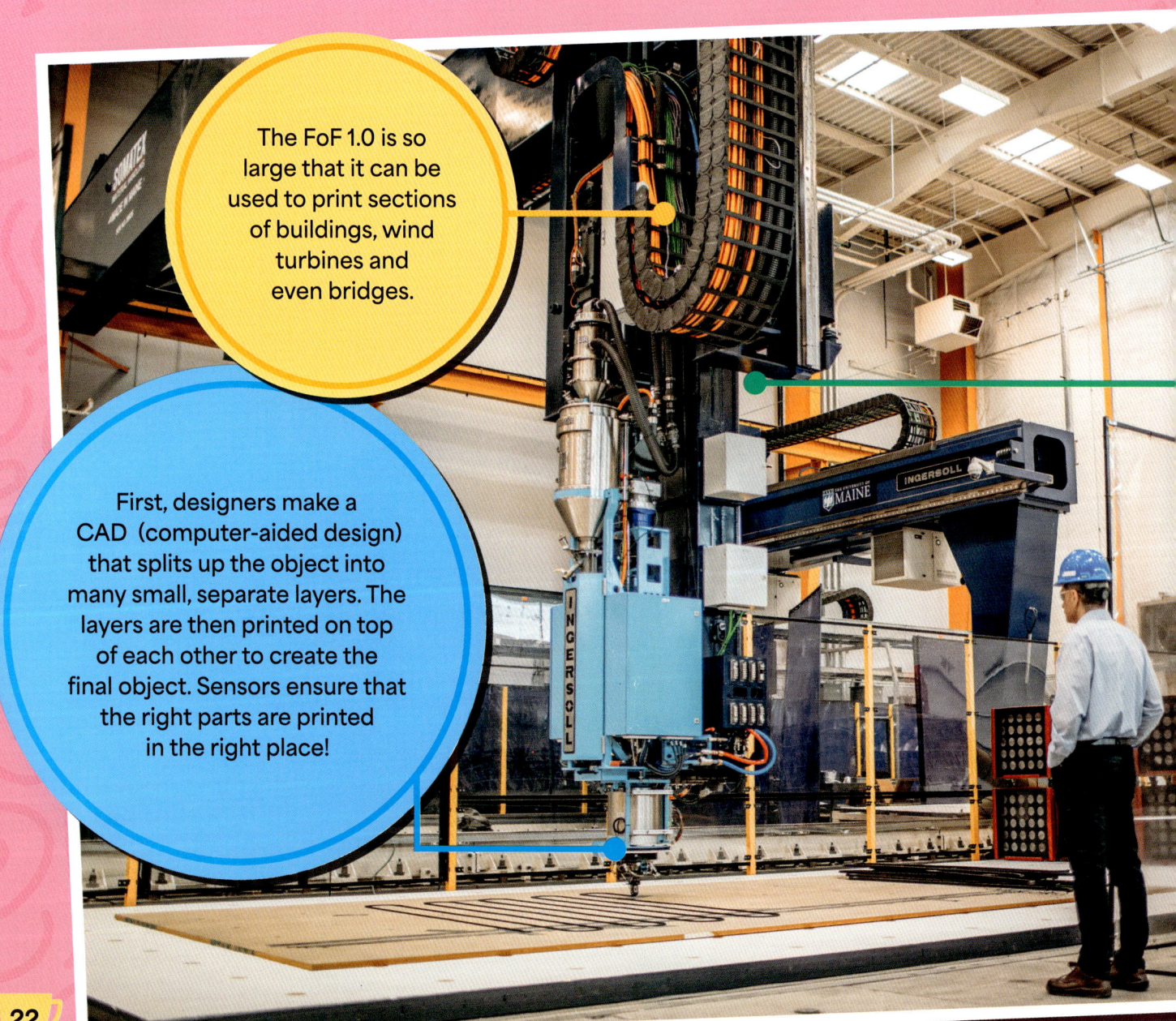

The FoF 1.0 is so large that it can be used to print sections of buildings, wind turbines and even bridges.

First, designers make a CAD (computer-aided design) that splits up the object into many small, separate layers. The layers are then printed on top of each other to create the final object. Sensors ensure that the right parts are printed in the right place!

PRINTING WITH PLASTIC

Most 3D printers (including the FoF 1.0) use thermoplastic as a printing material. This type of plastic is mouldable when heated but hardens as it cools. However, using new plastics isn't very sustainable, so the creators of the FoF 1.0 are experimenting with recycled plastics and even wood waste as alternative printing materials.

Its creators hope that the FoF 1.0 can be used to help create more affordable housing or with custom building repairs after natural disasters. It can print up to 227 kg of material per hour, so it wouldn't take long to print the pieces needed.

DID YOU KNOW?

3D-printed, plant-based 'salmon' is currently on sale in German supermarkets and other 3D-printed meals may be on our plates before too long!

I'm having an identity crisis!

REMOTE RESOURCE

3D printers are an incredible resource for people in remote areas, such as scientists in Antarctica or even astronauts in space! Rather than waiting for new parts or pieces to be delivered, they can simply design and print them themselves!

This astronaut is using a spanner that was 3D printed on the International Space Station (see pages 26-27).

Whizzy WiFi

FASTEST INTERNET SPEED

Videos left buffering? Websites not loading? Ever feel like your broadband is a little slow? Maybe you need to upgrade to the world's fastest Internet! With an incredible speed of **301 TERABITS PER SECOND**, it's 4.5 million times faster than the average home broadband.

Nowadays, wireless broadband is the most common type of home Internet. The Internet connection is sent to people's routers via fibre optic or telephone cables and then is shared wirelessly through the building via WiFi.

This record-breaking Internet speed was achieved by using the same standard fibre optic cables that many people have at home. Scientists created a device that unlocked a new wavelength in the cables, which allowed the signal to travel much faster than normal.

DID YOU KNOW?

With access to the fastest Internet speed, you could download every film ever made in just one minute!

🐌 Internet improvements

Internet speeds have already improved greatly over the past few decades. When dial-up Internet reached people's homes in the 1990s, it was around 18,000 times slower than our current standard Internet connection. A low-quality film would have taken over a day to download at full speed!

This means that it would be fairly easy for households to get super-speed Internet one day. We wouldn't need to replace any Internet cables - just get an unlocking device and change the frequency of our cables!

Dial-up Internet required the use of your home telephone line to access the Internet, which meant that you couldn't use the telephone and the Internet at the same time. Can you imagine?!

World wide web 🌐

Internet connection speed and access varies greatly around the world. Some low-income countries lack the infrastructure to deliver high-speed Internet connections to certain areas, particularly remote ones. However, new satellite Internet services such as Starlink can transmit Internet access to any part of the world from space, making it much easier for people in remote areas to get online.

Super SATELLITE

HEAVIEST ARTIFICIAL SATELLITE

As the largest space station ever built, it's no surprise that the **INTERNATIONAL SPACE STATION** (ISS) is the heaviest artificial satellite (object orbiting Earth), clocking in at a whopping 450,000 kg! But why does the ISS weigh so much and what stops it from crashing down back to Earth?

The ISS orbits Earth at just 400 km above its surface. It completes about 15 ½ orbits a day, with each orbit taking around 93 minutes in total.

The ISS contains many different areas and modules, including laboratories, sleeping and living areas for astronauts, storage space, generators and even robotic arms that can move objects in and out of the space station. With so many sections, it's no wonder it's so heavy!

WATER WEIGHT

The ISS also needs to carry enough water for its crew members to drink, cook and wash with, as well as extra water to turn into oxygen for the astronauts to breathe. Luckily, up to 98 per cent of the water brought from Earth can be recycled, so the ISS doesn't need to carry heavy backup water tanks.

On the ISS, wastewater from cooking and toilets (yuck!) and moisture from astronauts' breath and sweat is recycled so that it can be used again.

The ISS stays in orbit in spite of its weight because of its speed. It whizzes around Earth at approximately 8 km per second or 27,600 km per hour, which counteracts the force of gravity pulling it down to Earth.

DID YOU KNOW?

You can see the ISS in the night sky without using a telescope! Use the website on page 31 to track its movements and see if you can spot it.

HEADING DOWN

The ISS experiences friction as it moves through the atmosphere, which slowly pulls it closer to Earth at a rate of about 2 km per month. To keep the ISS nice and high in the sky, chemical fuel is used to drive it back up to its original altitude in space.

MORE INCREDIBLE

FASTEST TRAIN

The **L0 TRAIN** in Japan can reach a top speed of 603 km per hour, thanks to the power of magnets! Instead of rolling along on wheels, the L0 train levitates above the track, held in place by powerful electromagnets. This means that the train isn't slowed down by friction from the ground.

FASTEST PUZZLE-SOLVING ROBOT

Most people would need minutes, if not hours, to solve a puzzle cube, but not the **TOKUFASTBOT**. This record-breaking robot can rotate each part of the cube in just 0.009 seconds, allowing it to solve the puzzle in a staggering 0.305 seconds! The robot was built to highlight the super skill and speed of the company that supplied its parts.

SMALLEST MICROCHIP

The **IBM 2NM MICROCHIP** is as micro as a microchip can get! Each fingernail-sized chip contains an unbelievable 50 billion transistors, each containing parts narrower than a strand of DNA. The massive number of transistors on the microchip allows it to carry out tasks at great speed and store large amounts of data. Its small size means that even more microchips can be used within a computer, boosting its power even further.

You'd need to look through a microscope to see the transistors on the microchip!

TECHNOLOGY ★ RECORDS

MOST PROLIFIC INVENTOR

Every piece of technology is made up of many interconnecting parts, systems and software, many of which were designed and created by different people, who all hold patents for their designs. However, no one holds as many patents as the Japanese inventor **SHUNPEI YAMAZAKI**, who is responsible for over 11,000 different inventions! Most of his patents relate to computer displays.

OLDEST TECHNOLOGY

At first glance, these **STONE TOOLS** may not look like much compared to the advanced modern machines, but these unassuming pieces of stone are actually the first examples of technology. The use of these sophisticated tools to hunt and prepare food and materials marks the beginning of human history and the start of thousands of years of scientific progress and achievement.

LONGEST UNMANNED FLIGHT

The **ZEPHYR 8S** can spend over two months (64 days to be precise!) in the air without ever touching the ground! It is powered by solar energy and uses batteries to keep it running during the night. The unmanned vehicle can be used to monitor the environment or provide mobile phone coverage in hard-to-reach areas.

GLOSSARY

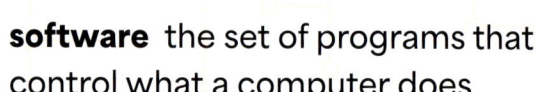

air resistance friction that acts on an object as it moves through the air

algorithm a set of rules or instructions for a computer to follow in order to complete a task

artificial created by humans

atom a very small particle

conduct to let electricity or heat pass through

friction a force that acts on an object moving across a surface

generator a machine that produces electricity

gravity a force that pulls things towards each other

infrared light a type of light that feels warm but can't be seen

orbit to follow a curved path around a planet or a star

program a series of instructions used to make a computer perform a task

software the set of programs that control what a computer does

sphere a 3D circle

streamlined describes something with a smooth shape

transistor a very small piece of electronic equipment used in computers and TVs

Further Information

Books

Stupendous and Tremendous Technology series by Sonya Newland and Claudia Martin
(Wayland, 2024)

Super Tech series by Clive Gifford and Chelen Écija
(Wayland, 2024)

The Wow and How of Technology by Cameron Menzies
(Wayland, 2024)

Websites

Discover 10 amazing technology facts
www.funkidslive.com/learn/top-10-facts-about-technology/

Learn more about how different technologies have developed throughout history
kids.britannica.com/kids/article/Technology-and-Invention/353296

Find out more about technology in space
spaceplace.nasa.gov/menu/science-and-technology/

Track the International Space Station as it orbits Earth
spotthestation.nasa.gov/tracking_map.cfm

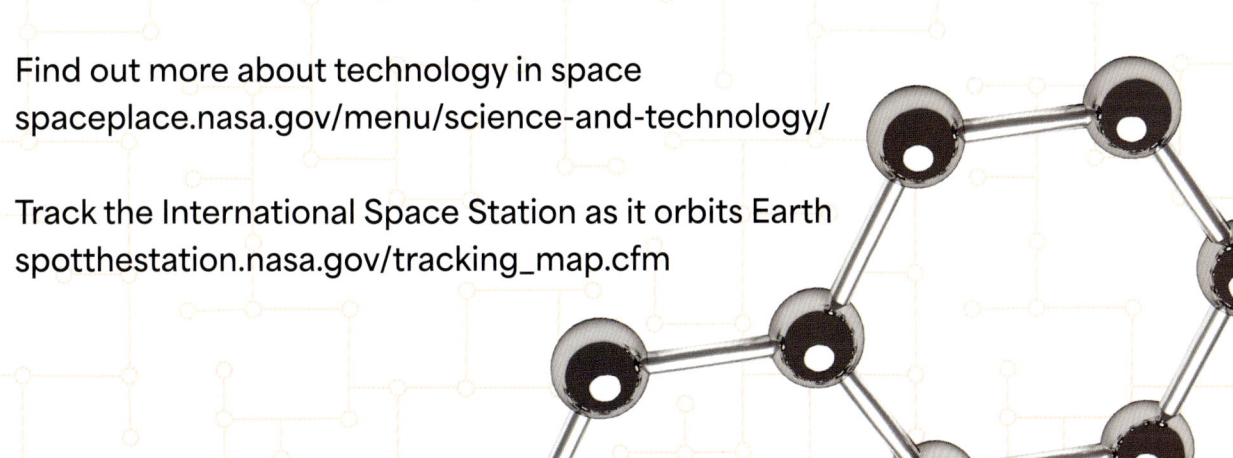

INDEX

3D printers 22-23

air resistance 16
algorithm 6, 7
Antonov An-225 4-5
atmosphere 17, 18, 27

Bhadla Solar Park 14-15

data 7, 12, 19, 28
Deepsea Challenger 8-9

electricity 11, 13, 14, 15, 21
engines 4, 16, 17

FoF 1.0 3D printer 22-23
friction 27, 28
Frontier supercomputer 12-13

graphene 10-11
gravity 27

heat 13, 19, 23

IBM 2nm microchip 28
International Space Station 23, 26-27
Internet 6, 24-25

James Webb Space Telescope 18-19

L0 train 28
light 8, 14, 18, 19

materials 9, 10, 11, 19, 20, 23
mirrors 19

patents 29
pressure 9

radiation 17
Robobee 20-21
robots 15, 20, 21, 26, 28

satellites 15, 25, 26, 27
search engines 6-7
sensors 11, 22
solar power 14, 15, 29
sound barrier 16
spacecraft 4, 17, 18, 19, 23, 25, 26, 27
speed 16, 17, 28
stone tools 29

ThrustSSC 16-17
Tokufastbot 28

water 8, 9, 11, 13, 15, 21, 27
websites 6, 24
wings 4, 5, 20, 21

Yamazaki, Shunpei 29

Zephyr 8S 29

TITLES IN THE SERIES

- Sprint at speed
- Champion snoozer
- Mighty muncher
- Harmful hunter
- Top twister
- Powerful poison
- Cool climber
- Underwater roar
- Need for speed
- Super furry animal
- Marathon migrator
- Skilled sniffer
- More incredible animal records

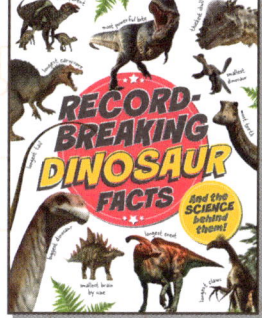

- Diverse dinos
- Bone-crushing bite
- Baby brain
- Claw-some lengths
- Small-o-saurus
- Too many teeth?
- Sturdy skulls
- Number one dino
- Tail titan
- Mum's the word
- Crest champion
- Bonkers big
- More incredible dinosaur records

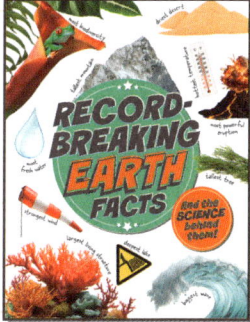

- Explosive eruption
- Wave power
- Dusty and dry
- So many species
- Speedy breeze
- Mighty mountain
- Cool as ice
- Burn, baby, burn
- Champion coral
- Dark depths
- Waterfall wonder
- Plant power
- More incredible Earth records

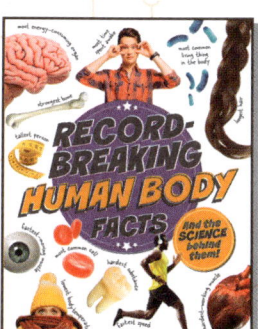

- Prize-winning pumping
- Feeling sleepy?
- Brain drain
- Almost freezing
- Mega-fast muscle
- So many cells
- Not so small
- Deep breath in ...
- Hard as a ... tooth?
- Rocket-powered run
- Baby bones
- Body invaders
- More incredible human body records

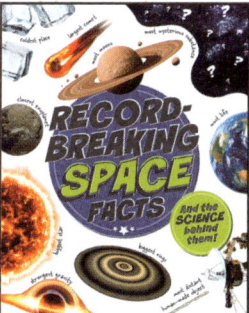

- A real superstar
- Short days
- Far, far away
- A powerful pull
- Roaming robots
- Mega rings
- Alive and kicking
- Space neighbour
- Strange substance
- Hot and cold
- So many moons
- Life lift-off
- More incredible space records

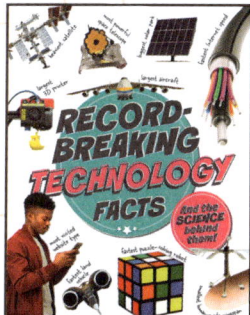

- Too big to fly?
- Champion clicks
- Deep, deep down
- Solid and sturdy
- Prize processors
- Let it shine
- (Nearly!) supersonic speed
- Seeing in space
- Fabulous fliers
- King of the printers
- Whizzy WiFi
- Super satellite
- More incredible technology records